THE INDIAN TEXTILE

AN INSIGHT INTO THE RICH HISTORY AND DIVERSITY OF INDIAN TEXTILE TRADITIONS

DR. JAGADEESH PILLAI

|| "Dedicated to all who seek to understand and appreciate Indian culture and tradition." ||

Contents

Contents

Prayer

**"Om Bhadram Karnebhih Shrunuyaama
DevaahBhadram Pashyemaakshabhiryajatraah
SthirairangaistushtuvaamsastanoobhihVyashema
Devahitam YadaayuhSwasti Na Indro
VridhashravaahSwasti Nah Pooshaa
VishwavedaahSwasti Nastaarkshyo ArishtanemihSwasti
No Brihaspatir DadhaatuOm Shantih, Shantih, Shantih"**

The literal meaning of this mantra is: OM. O Gods! Let us
hear auspicious words from our ears. O reverent Gods! Let
us behold propitious visions from our eyes, let our organs
and body be stable, healthy, and strong. Let us do that
which is pleasing to the gods in the life span allotted to us.
May Indra, inscribed in the scriptures, bring us fortune!
May Pushan, the knower of the world, grant us prosperity!
May Trakshya, who vanquishes enemies, bestow us with
blessings! May Brihaspati bring us success!
OM Peace, Peace, Peace.

About The Author

Dr. Jagadeesh Pillai is a renowned Guinness World Record holder, writer, and researcher hailing from Varanasi, also known as the abode of Lord Shiva. With a Ph.D. in Vedic Science and a range of creative ideas and achievements, he is a true polymath. He is the author of more than 100 books including Research Publications. Although his roots can be traced back to Kerala, the people of Varanasi hold him in high regard and affectionately consider him one of their own.

Dr. Pillai has achieved four Guinness World Records in the following subjects:

"Script to Screen" - In this record, Dr. Pillai produced and directed an animation film within the shortest time possible, breaking the previous record set by Canadians. He has also received numerous national and international awards and recognitions for this achievement.

Longest Line of Postcards - For this record, Dr. Pillai created a line of 16,300 postcards on the occasion of the 163rd anniversary of Indian Postal Day. The event also included a questionnaire about the Indian flag.

Largest Poster Awareness Campaign - Dr. Pillai designed an awareness campaign on the subject of "Beti Bachao - Beti Padhao" (Save the Girl Child - Educate the Girl Child) to achieve this record.

Largest Envelope - In tribute to the Indian Prime Minister's

"Make in India" initiative, Dr. Pillai created a 4000 square meter envelope using waste paper to achieve this record.

Attempted - **70000 Candles on a 210 kg Cake** - To celebrate the 70th Indian Independence Day, Dr. Pillai attempted to light 70,000 candles on a 210 kg cake, which was recorded in World Records India.

Attempted - **Documentary on Dhamek Stupa of Sarnath in 17 Languages** - Dr. Pillai attempted to create a documentary on the Dhamek Stupa of Sarnath, dubbing it in 17 different languages. The result of this attempt is currently awaiting confirmation from the Guinness World Records.

Dr. Pillai is skilled in teaching the Bhagavad Gita, a Hindu scripture, and is popular among young people. He has helped many young people improve their lives through his motivational teachings.

In addition to teaching, he has composed and sung numerous Sanskrit Bhajans and patriotic songs.

He has also written and directed several short films and documentaries for awareness campaigns, and has volunteered with the police in both UP and Kerala to spread awareness about various issues through videos and photography.

Incredibly, he has produced and directed over 100 documentaries about the city of Varanasi, all on his own.

He has also helped and guided more than 25 boys and girls to achieve world records through creative and innovative methods. He is a multifaceted person who uses his intellect and the blessings given to him by God to excel in various areas. He is both a teacher and a student, always learning and teaching, and is able to master any subject he comes across.

He is a selfless social activist and motivational speaker who has overcome struggles and failures to become a successful and enthusiastic individual with a rich life experience.

In addition to his work with the Bhagavad Gita, he is also an efficient Tarot card reader, Astro-Vastu consultant, and a talented singer and composer. He has sung the entire Ram Charita Manas and Bhagavad Gita in his own compositions, and has sung the phrase "Lokah Samastha Sukhino Bhavantu" in 50 different languages. He is currently working on a detailed and scientific study of Vedas, Upanishads, Puranas, and the Bhagavad Gita. He has also composed and sung the Hanuman Chalisa and Gayatri Mantra in 108 and 1008 different compositions, respectively.

Awards - Four Times Guinness World Records, Winner of Mahatma Gandhi Vishwa Shanti Puraskar, Mahatma Gandhi Global Peace Ambassador, Kashi Ratna Award, Dr. APJ Abdul Kalam Motivational Person of the Year 2017, Mother Teresa Award, Indira Gandhi Priyadarshini Award, Bharat Vikas Ratna Award, Udyog Ratna Award, Vigyan Prasar Award, Poorvanchal Ratn Samman.

PREFACE

The Indian textile industry is a rich tapestry of history, tradition, and culture. The industry has played a significant role in the country's economy and society for centuries, and continues to do so to this day. This book, **"Threads of Tradition: Exploring the History and Diversity of Indian Textiles"** delves into the complex and diverse world of Indian textiles, exploring its history, current state, and future potential.

From the ancient techniques and designs of the handloom and handicraft sector, to the modern innovations of the organized textile industry, this book provides a comprehensive look at the Indian textile industry. It covers the major markets and export destinations for Indian textiles, as well as the government policies and programs that support and promote the industry.

This book also explores the use of Indian textiles in contemporary art and fashion, highlighting the ongoing significance of the industry in preserving and promoting India's cultural heritage. The book is intended for anyone interested in understanding the Indian textile industry, from its rich history and diverse traditions to its current state and future potential.

The book is divided into chapters that cover various aspects of the Indian textile industry, providing a detailed and comprehensive understanding of the subject. The authors have used their expertise and extensive research to provide readers with a comprehensive and informative look at the

Indian textile industry.

We hope that this book will be a valuable resource for anyone interested in understanding the Indian textile industry and its ongoing significance in the country's economy, culture, and art.

I

Introduction: Understanding the Indian Textile

The Indian textile industry is one of the oldest and most diverse in the world. From the handwoven fabrics of the Indus Valley Civilization to the modern textile mills of today, India has a rich history and tradition of textile production. In this chapter, we will explore the various aspects of the Indian textile industry, including its history, traditional techniques, and current state.

The history of Indian textiles can be traced back to the Indus Valley Civilization, which existed around 2500 BCE. Excavations of Indus Valley sites have revealed that the people of this civilization were skilled in spinning and weaving cotton, as well as dyeing the fibers with natural dyes. The use of these natural dyes can be seen in the vibrant colors of the fabrics that have been discovered at

Indus Valley sites.

During the medieval period, Indian textiles were highly sought after by traders from around the world. The Mughal emperors, in particular, were known for their patronage of the textile industry, and Indian fabrics were exported to Europe, the Middle East, and Southeast Asia. The traditional techniques used in Indian textile production, such as handlooms and block printing, were passed down from generation to generation and continue to be used today.

One of the most unique aspect of Indian textile is the diversity that can be seen in different regions. Each state and region of India has its own distinct textile traditions and techniques, which are influenced by the local culture, climate, and available resources. For example, the handloom textiles of the southern state of Tamil Nadu are known for their intricate designs and use of natural dyes, while the textile traditions of the western state of Gujarat are characterized by their use of vibrant colors and intricate embroidery.

The traditional techniques of Indian textile production are still widely used today, particularly in rural areas. However, the industry has also modernized in recent years, with the emergence of large textile mills and the use of modern machinery. Despite this modernization, the traditional techniques are still an important part of the Indian textile industry and are valued for their unique characteristics and cultural significance.

The Indian textile industry is a rich and diverse field that has a long history and tradition. From the ancient Indus Valley Civilization to the modern textile mills of today, India has a unique textile heritage that is shaped by its local culture, climate, and available resources. The traditional techniques of Indian textile production are an important part of this heritage and continue to be valued for their unique characteristics and cultural significance.

"The Indian textile industry is a rich tapestry of history, tradition, and culture."

⊗

II

The Ancient Indian Textile: Indus Valley Civilization and Vedic Period

The ancient Indian textile industry can be traced back to the Indus Valley Civilization, which existed around 2500 BCE. Excavations of Indus Valley sites have revealed that the people of this civilization were skilled in spinning and weaving cotton, as well as dyeing the fibers with natural dyes. The use of these natural dyes can be seen in the vibrant colors of the fabrics that have been discovered at Indus Valley sites. The Indus Valley civilization also had a complex system of weights and measures, indicating a sophisticated textile trade.

The Vedic Period, which followed the Indus Valley Civilization, also had a rich tradition of textile production.

The Vedic texts, such as the Rigveda, mention the use of cotton and silk, as well as the use of dyeing and weaving techniques. The Vedic people were also skilled in spinning, and the spinning wheel is mentioned in the Vedic texts as a symbol of wealth and prosperity.

During the Vedic period, textiles were used for a variety of purposes, including clothing, household items, and religious offerings. The use of textiles was also an important aspect of social and economic life, as textiles were used as a form of currency and as a way to demonstrate wealth and status.

Overall, the ancient Indian textile industry was advanced and sophisticated, with a long history and tradition of textile production. The Indus Valley Civilization and Vedic Period were significant in the development of the Indian textile industry, and their textile traditions continue to influence the industry today.

"The Indian textile industry has played a significant role in the country's economy and society for centuries."

છ

III

The Traditional Textile-making Techniques in India

India has a rich tradition of textile production, and many traditional techniques are still used today. Some of the most common traditional textile-making techniques in India include:

Handloom Weaving: Handloom weaving is one of the oldest textile-making techniques in India. It involves using a hand-operated loom to weave fabric. Handloom weaving is particularly common in rural areas and is known for producing high-quality, unique fabrics.

Block Printing: Block printing is a traditional printing technique that involves using carved wooden blocks to apply designs to fabric. This technique is commonly used to create intricate patterns and designs on fabrics such as cotton and silk.

Tie-Dyeing: Tie-dyeing, also known as Bandhani, is a traditional dyeing technique that involves tying small portions of fabric in a specific pattern before immersing the fabric in dye. This technique is commonly used to create unique designs and patterns on fabrics such as cotton and silk.

Embroidery: Embroidery is a decorative technique that involves stitching designs onto fabric. It is a traditional art form that is widely practiced in India and is used to create intricate and beautiful designs on fabrics such as cotton and silk.

Zari Work: Zari work is a traditional technique that involves using a thin metal thread to create intricate designs on fabrics. Zari work is commonly used on fabrics such as silk and is associated with the Indian state of Gujarat.

Kantha: Kantha is a traditional embroidery technique that is practiced in India, particularly in the eastern state of West Bengal. It involves running a simple running stitch along the edges of a piece of fabric to create a decorative design.

These traditional textile-making techniques are an important part of Indian culture and are valued for their unique characteristics and cultural significance. Many of these techniques are passed down from generation to generation and continue to be used today, particularly in rural areas.

"Indian textiles are known for their unique designs and intricate patterns, an important aspect of India's cultural heritage."

⁜

IV

Regional Textile Traditions of India: North, South, East, and West

India is a diverse country with a rich tradition of textile production. Each region of India has its own distinct textile traditions and techniques that are influenced by the local culture, climate, and available resources. Here's an overview of some of the regional textile traditions of India:

North: The northern region of India is known for its rich textile traditions, particularly in states such as Uttar Pradesh, Gujarat, and Rajasthan. The traditional fabrics of this region include cotton, silk, and wool, and are known for their intricate designs and vibrant colors. The traditional techniques used in this region include handloom weaving, block printing, and embroidery. The famous Banarasi silk sarees and the traditional fabrics of Gujarat such as Patola, Bandhini, and Kota Doria are famous from this region.

South: The southern region of India is known for its handloom textiles, particularly in states such as Tamil Nadu, Kerala, and Andhra Pradesh. The traditional fabrics of this region include cotton, silk, and chiffon, and are known for their intricate designs and use of natural dyes. The traditional techniques used in this region include handloom weaving, tie-dyeing, and embroidery. The famous Kanjeevaram and Ilkal sarees are famous from this region.

East: The eastern region of India is known for its traditional fabrics, particularly in states such as West Bengal, Odisha, and Assam. The traditional fabrics of this region include cotton, silk, and muslin, and are known for their use of natural dyes and intricate designs. The traditional techniques used in this region include handloom weaving, block printing, and embroidery. The famous Tant sarees and the traditional fabrics of Assam such as Muga silk are famous from this region.

West: The western region of India is known for its traditional fabrics, particularly in states such as Gujarat, Maharashtra, and Rajasthan. The traditional fabrics of this region include cotton, silk, and wool, and are known for their use of vibrant colors and intricate embroidery. The traditional techniques used in this region include handloom weaving, tie-dyeing, and embroidery. The famous Paithani sarees and the traditional fabrics of Gujarat such as Patola, Bandhini, and Kota Doria are famous from this region.

Each region of India has its own unique textile traditions and techniques that are influenced by the local culture, climate, and available resources. These regional textile traditions are an important part of Indian culture and are valued for their unique characteristics and cultural significance.

"The Indian textile industry continues to be of ongoing significance for the Indian economy, culture and art scene."

ॐ

V

The Handloom Textiles of India

Handloom textiles are a traditional and important part of the Indian textile industry. Handloom weaving is a process in which fabric is woven on a hand-operated loom. The handlooms in India are classified into two types - pit loom and frame loom. Handloom textiles are known for their unique designs, high quality, and cultural significance.

Handloom textiles are particularly common in rural areas of India, where many artisans continue to practice this traditional craft. Each region of India has its own unique handloom textiles that are influenced by the local culture, climate, and available resources. For example, the handloom textiles of the southern state of Tamil Nadu are known for their intricate designs and use of natural dyes, while the handloom textiles of the eastern state of West Bengal are known for their use of lightweight cotton fabrics and intricate embroidery.

Handloom textiles are made from a variety of natural fibers, including cotton, silk, and wool. The traditional techniques used in handloom textile production include spinning, dyeing, and weaving. These techniques are passed down from generation to generation and are an important part of the Indian textile heritage.

Handloom textiles play an important role in the Indian economy, particularly in rural areas. They provide employment and income for many artisans and their families. The Government of India has initiated various schemes to support the handloom sector and promote traditional textiles, such as the Handloom Mark and the Handloom Weavers' Comprehensive Welfare Scheme.

Handloom textiles are an integral part of the Indian textile industry and culture. They are known for their unique designs, high quality, and cultural significance. Handloom textiles are particularly common in rural areas, where many artisans continue to practice this traditional craft, and play an important role in the Indian economy.

"The traditional techniques and designs of the Indian textile industry are passed down through generations."

☙

VI

The Silk Textiles of India

Silk textiles are an important part of the Indian textile industry. India has a long history of silk production and is one of the major silk-producing countries in the world. Silk is a luxurious and versatile natural fiber that is valued for its softness, strength, and shine.

The silk textiles of India are known for their unique designs, high quality, and cultural significance. Silk fabrics are produced in various regions of India, each with its own unique characteristics and techniques. Some of the famous silk textiles of India are:

Banarasi silk: Banarasi silk is a traditional silk textile that is produced in the city of Varanasi in Uttar Pradesh, North India. It is known for its intricate designs, gold and silver threadwork, and use of vibrant colors. Banarasi silk is used to make sarees, dupattas and other traditional garments.

Kanjeevaram silk: Kanjeevaram silk is a traditional silk textile that is produced in the city of Kanchipuram in Tamil Nadu, South India. It is known for its bright colors, gold threadwork and use of zari. Kanjeevaram silk is mainly used to make sarees.

Paithani silk: Paithani silk is a traditional silk textile that is produced in the city of Paithan in Maharashtra, West India. It is known for its intricate designs, vibrant colors, and gold threadwork. Paithani silk is mainly used to make sarees.

Muga silk: Muga silk is a traditional silk textile that is produced in the state of Assam, East India. It is known for its natural golden color, durability, and softness. Muga silk is mainly used to make sarees and traditional garments.

Silk textiles are an important part of the Indian economy, particularly in rural areas. They provide employment and income for many artisans and their families. The Government of India has initiated various schemes to support the silk sector and promote traditional silk textiles, such as the Silk Mark and the Integrated Scheme for Development of Silk Industry.

Silk textiles are an integral part of the Indian textile industry and culture. They are known for their unique designs, high quality, and cultural significance. Silk textiles are produced in various regions of India, each with its own unique characteristics and techniques, and play an important role in the Indian economy.

ॐ

"The Indian textile industry is a major contributor to the country's economy, with an estimated 45 million people employed in the sector."

ॐ

VII
The Cotton Textiles of India

Cotton textiles are an important part of the Indian textile industry. India has a long history of cotton production and is one of the major cotton-producing countries in the world. Cotton is a versatile natural fiber that is valued for its breathability, durability, and softness.

The cotton textiles of India are known for their unique designs, high quality, and cultural significance. Cotton fabrics are produced in various regions of India, each with its own unique characteristics and techniques. Some of the famous cotton textiles of India are:

Khadi: Khadi is a traditional handspun and handwoven cotton textile that is produced in various regions of India. It is known for its natural colors, rough texture, and use of traditional techniques. Khadi is used to make garments such as kurtas, sarees, and dhotis.

Chikankari: Chikankari is a traditional embroidery technique that is applied to cotton fabrics. It is mainly produced in the city of Lucknow, in the state of Uttar Pradesh, North India. Chikankari is known for its delicate and intricate designs, and is used to make garments such as kurtas, sarees, and salwar kameez.

Kota Doria: Kota Doria is a traditional cotton textile that is produced in the city of Kota, in the state of Rajasthan, West India. It is known for its lightweight, sheer fabric and use of traditional weaving techniques. Kota Doria is mainly used to make sarees and dupattas.

Handloom cotton: Handloom cotton textiles are produced in various regions of India. They are known for their unique designs, high quality and use of traditional techniques. Handloom cotton is mainly used to make garments such as sarees, dhotis and lungis.

Cotton textiles are an important part of the Indian economy, particularly in rural areas. They provide employment and income for many artisans and their families. The Government of India has initiated various schemes to support the cotton sector and promote traditional cotton textiles, such as the National Handloom Development Programme and the Technology Upgradation Fund Scheme.

Cotton textiles are an integral part of the Indian textile industry and culture. They are known for their unique designs, high quality, and cultural significance. Cotton textiles are produced in various regions of India, each with its own unique characteristics and techniques, and play an important role in the Indian economy.

"The use of textiles as an art medium highlights the rich cultural and traditional heritage of India."

ଔ

VIII
The Tribal Textiles of India

Tribal textiles are an important part of the Indian textile industry and culture. The tribal communities of India have a rich tradition of textile production that is influenced by their local culture, climate, and available resources. The textiles produced by these communities are known for their unique designs, high quality, and cultural significance.

Tribal textiles are produced in various regions of India, each with its own unique characteristics and techniques. Some of the famous tribal textiles of India are:

Warli: Warli textiles are produced by the Warli tribe of Maharashtra, West India. They are known for their simple geometric designs and use of natural dyes. Warli textiles are mainly used to make garments such as skirts and shawls.

Gond: Gond textiles are produced by the Gond tribe of

Madhya Pradesh, Central India. They are known for their vibrant colors and use of traditional dyeing and printing techniques. Gond textiles are mainly used to make garments such as skirts and shawls.

Bhutia: Bhutia textiles are produced by the Bhutia tribe of Sikkim, Northeast India. They are known for their intricate designs and use of traditional weaving techniques. Bhutia textiles are mainly used to make garments such as shawls, scarves, and bags.

Toda: Toda textiles are produced by the Toda tribe of Tamil Nadu, South India. They are known for their use of traditional dyeing and weaving techniques and are used to make garments such as shawls and dhotis.

Tribal textiles are an important part of the Indian economy, particularly in rural areas. They provide employment and income for many artisans and their families. The Government of India has initiated various schemes to support the tribal textile sector and promote traditional tribal textiles, such as the Development of Indigenous Textile Industry and the Scheme for Development of Silk and Silk Textile Industry.

Tribal textiles are an integral part of the Indian textile industry and culture. They are known for their unique designs, high quality, and cultural significance. Tribal textiles are produced in various regions of India, each with its own unique characteristics and techniques, and play an important role in the Indian economy.

*"The Indian government has implemented
various policies and programs to support and
promote the textile industry."*

୫

IX

The Indian Textile in Fashion and Design

The Indian textile industry has had a significant influence on fashion and design. Indian textiles are known for their unique designs, high quality, and cultural significance, which makes them a popular choice in the fashion and design industry.

One of the ways Indian textiles are used in fashion and design is through the use of traditional techniques and natural dyes. Many traditional Indian textile-making techniques, such as handloom weaving, block printing, and tie-dyeing, are now being used in the fashion and design industry to create unique and sustainable textiles. The use of natural dyes, which is a common practice in India, is also becoming increasingly popular in the fashion and design industry as a way to produce eco-friendly and sustainable textiles.

Indian textiles are also used in fashion and design to create unique and diverse garments. Indian fashion designers often use Indian textiles such as silk, cotton, and handloom to create traditional garments like sarees, lehengas and kurtas, as well as contemporary clothing like dresses and jackets. Indian textiles are known for their intricate designs and vibrant colors, which makes them a popular choice for creating unique and eye-catching garments.

Indian textile and fashion designers are increasingly getting recognition globally. The Indian textile and fashion industry is getting global recognition through participation in international fashion shows and exhibitions. Many Indian textile and fashion designers are showing their collections in international fashion shows and exhibitions and are gaining recognition for their unique and diverse designs.

The Indian textile industry has had a significant influence on fashion and design. Indian textiles are known for their unique designs, high quality, and cultural significance, which makes them a popular choice in the fashion and design industry. Indian textile and fashion designers are increasingly getting recognition globally, with many showcasing their collections in international fashion shows and exhibitions.

୫୭

"The major markets for Indian textile exports include the United States, the European Union, and China."

೮೦

X

The Influence of Indian Textile on World Textile Industry

The Indian textile industry has had a significant influence on the world textile industry. India has a long history of textile production and is known for its rich tradition of textile production. The textiles produced in India are known for their unique designs, high quality, and cultural significance.

One of the ways India has influenced the world textile industry is through its use of traditional techniques and natural dyes. Many traditional Indian textile-making techniques, such as handloom weaving, block printing, and tie-dyeing, are now being adopted by textile industries around the world. The use of natural dyes, which is a common practice in India, is also becoming increasingly popular in the global textile industry as a way to produce eco-friendly and sustainable textiles.

Another way India has influenced the world textile industry is through its exports of textiles. India is one of the world's largest exporters of textiles, and its textiles are in high demand around the world. Indian textiles are known for their unique designs, high quality, and cultural significance, which has led to a growing interest in Indian textiles in the global market.

India's textile industry also has a strong impact on the fashion industry. Indian textile and fashion designers are increasingly getting recognition globally and their designs are being featured in international fashion shows. Indian fabrics and textiles such as silk, cotton and handloom are being used by famous international fashion designers in their collections.

The Indian textile industry has had a significant influence on the world textile industry. Its use of traditional techniques and natural dyes, as well as its exports of textiles, has led to a growing interest in Indian textiles in the global market. India's textile industry also has a strong impact on the fashion industry, with Indian textile and fashion designers increasingly getting recognition globally.

"The Indian textile industry also plays a vital role in the country's contemporary art scene."

৩

XI

The Impact of Modernization on Indian Textile

The Indian textile industry has a rich history dating back to ancient times. Traditional techniques and designs have been passed down through generations, with each region of India developing its own unique style. However, with the advent of modernization and globalization, the Indian textile industry has undergone significant changes.

One of the most notable impacts of modernization on the Indian textile industry is the increased use of mechanization and automation. This has led to a significant increase in production efficiency and output, allowing textile manufacturers to meet the demands of both domestic and international markets. However, it has also led to the displacement of traditional artisans and the loss of traditional techniques and designs.

Another impact of modernization is the increased use of synthetic materials, such as polyester and nylon, in the production of textiles. These materials are cheaper and more readily available than traditional natural fibers such as cotton and silk. This has led to a decline in the use of traditional materials and techniques, and a shift towards mass production of textiles.

The increased competition and global market pressures have also led to a decline in the quality of Indian textiles. In order to compete with cheaper imports, many textile manufacturers have been forced to cut costs by using lower quality materials and production methods. This has led to a decline in the reputation of Indian textiles, which were once known for their high quality and durability.

However, it is not all negative, modernization has also brought significant benefits to the Indian textile industry. The increasing use of technology has led to the development of new and innovative designs, and the ability to produce textiles on a larger scale has increased the accessibility of Indian textiles to a wider audience. The textile industry has also seen a renewed interest in traditional techniques and designs, as consumers become more conscious of the importance of preserving cultural heritage.

In recent years, the government has also taken steps to promote the growth and development of the Indian textile industry. Measures such as the National Handloom Development Programme and the National Handicrafts and Handlooms Museum have been implemented to promote traditional techniques and designs, and to provide support for artisans and small scale textile manufacturers.

Modernization has had a significant impact on the Indian textile industry. While it has brought increased efficiency and accessibility, it has also led to the displacement of traditional artisans and the loss of traditional techniques and designs. However, with the renewed interest in traditional techniques and designs and the support of the government, the Indian textile industry has the potential to continue to thrive and evolve in the modern world, preserving the rich heritage and diversity of Indian textile traditions.

"The Indian textile industry has a rich history
and diverse traditions that have played a
significant role in the country's economy and
culture."

છ

XII

The Conservation and Preservation of Indian Textile Heritage

The conservation and preservation of Indian textile heritage is of paramount importance in order to ensure that the rich traditions and techniques of Indian textile-making are not lost to future generations. This can be achieved through a variety of means, including:

Museums and exhibitions: Museums and exhibitions play a vital role in preserving and showcasing Indian textile heritage. These institutions collect, preserve, and display a wide range of textiles, including traditional garments, fabrics, and embellishments. They also provide educational opportunities for visitors to learn about the history and cultural significance of Indian textiles.

Documentation and Research: Documentation and research are crucial for understanding and preserving Indian textile heritage. This includes the documentation of traditional techniques, designs, and materials, as well as the study of the cultural and historical context of Indian textiles. This information can be used to inform conservation and restoration efforts, as well as to provide a deeper understanding of Indian textile heritage.

Training and Education: Training and education are important for ensuring that traditional textile-making techniques are passed down to future generations. This includes the training of artisans in traditional techniques, as well as the education of textile conservators and curators. This helps to ensure that traditional textile-making skills are not lost, and that Indian textile heritage is preserved for future generations.

Government Support: Government support is important in order to ensure the preservation and promotion of Indian textile heritage. This includes the establishment of policies and programmes that support traditional textile-making techniques, as well as the allocation of funding for conservation and restoration efforts. The government can also provide support for artisans and small-scale textile manufacturers, helping to ensure that traditional textile-making skills are not lost.

Community Engagement: Community engagement is a key aspect of preserving Indian textile heritage. This includes working with local communities to document and preserve traditional textile-making techniques, as well as promoting the use of traditional textiles in daily life. This helps to ensure that traditional textile-making skills are not lost, and that Indian textile heritage is preserved for future generations.

The conservation and preservation of Indian textile heritage is a complex and ongoing process that requires the efforts of a wide range of stakeholders, including museums, researchers, artisans, government, and local communities. By working together, we can ensure that the rich traditions and techniques of Indian textile-making are not lost to future generations and that Indian textile heritage is preserved for future generations to appreciate and learn from.

"Indian textile industry continues to preserve
the traditional textile practices and
techniques."

೮೦

XIII

The Indian Textile in Trade and Export

The Indian textile industry has a rich history and diverse traditions that have been passed down through generations. The industry has played a significant role in the country's economy, with a large portion of its output being exported to other countries. India is one of the largest producers of cotton and silk, and is also known for its production of handloom and handicraft textiles. The country's textile exports include a wide range of products such as cotton yarn, fabrics, made-ups, and garments.

The Indian textile industry can be traced back to ancient times, when India was known for its high-quality textiles that were in high demand by traders and merchants from around the world. The industry continued to thrive during the Mughal era, with the development of new techniques and the introduction of new materials. The British colonial period also had a significant impact on the industry, with the introduction of new machinery and the establishment of textile mills.

Today, the Indian textile industry is a major contributor to the country's economy, with an estimated 45 million people employed in the sector. The industry is divided into two main segments: the organized sector and the unorganized sector. The organized sector includes large textile mills and factories, while the unorganized sector includes small-scale cottage industries and home-based workers.

The major markets for Indian textile exports include the United States, the European Union, and China. The United States is the largest market for Indian textile exports, accounting for around 25% of the total exports. The European Union is the second-largest market, accounting for around 15% of the total exports. China is also a significant market for Indian textile exports, with a growing demand for Indian textiles in the country.

The Indian government has implemented various policies and programs to support and promote the textile industry. The Scheme for Integrated Textile Parks, for example, aims to provide infrastructure and common facilities to textile units, with the goal of increasing productivity and competitiveness. The Technology Upgradation Fund Scheme is another initiative that provides financial assistance to textile units for upgrading their technology and increasing their competitiveness.

The Indian textile industry is also known for its handloom

and handicraft textiles, which are produced in various regions across the country. These textiles are known for their unique designs and intricate patterns, and are in high demand by buyers from around the world. The Indian government has also implemented various programs to promote the handloom and handicraft sector, including the National Handloom Development Program and the Handloom Weavers' Comprehensive Welfare Scheme.

The Indian textile industry has a rich history and diverse traditions that have played a significant role in the country's economy. The industry is a major contributor to the country's economy, with a large portion of its output being exported to other countries. The Indian government has implemented various policies and programs to support and promote the textile industry, including the Scheme for Integrated Textile Parks and the Technology Upgradation Fund Scheme. The industry is also known for its handloom and handicraft textiles, which are produced in various regions across the country and are in high demand by buyers from around the world.

"The Indian textile industry is divided into two main segments: the organized sector and the unorganized sector."

⁗

XIV

The Indian Textile in Contemporary Art

The Indian textile industry has also played a significant role in contemporary art in India. Many Indian artists have used textiles as a medium for their work, incorporating traditional techniques and designs into their pieces. This can be seen in the use of traditional Indian fabrics such as silk, cotton, and khadi in painting and mixed-media art.

One notable example is the work of artist Nalini Malani, who is known for her large-scale installations that incorporate traditional Indian textile techniques such as hand-painted and block-printed fabrics. Similarly, artist Jitish Kallat is known for his use of traditional Indian textiles in his mixed-media works, often incorporating fabrics into his paintings and sculptures.

In recent years, there has been a growing interest in the use of traditional Indian textiles in contemporary fashion and design. Designers such as Sabyasachi Mukherjee and Ritu Kumar have gained international recognition for their use of traditional Indian fabrics and techniques in their collections. These designers often incorporate traditional Indian textile motifs and patterns into their designs, giving them a distinct and unique aesthetic.

The Indian textile industry also plays a vital role in the country's contemporary art scene, as textile is a medium that can be used to communicate cultural, political, and social messages. The use of textiles as an art medium highlights the rich cultural and traditional heritage of India and also helps to preserve traditional textile practices and techniques.

Indian textile industry has been a significant part of contemporary art in India and has been used as a medium by artists to communicate cultural, political, and social messages. The traditional techniques and designs are incorporated into the contemporary art pieces and fashion, giving them a unique aesthetic. The use of textiles as an art medium highlights the rich cultural and traditional heritage of India and also helps to preserve traditional textile practices and techniques.

"Indian textiles are known for their unique designs and intricate patterns, and are in high demand by buyers from around the world."

৵

XV

The Ongoing Significance of Indian Textile

The Indian textile industry has a rich history and diverse traditions that have played a significant role in the country's economy and culture. The industry continues to be a major contributor to the country's economy, with a large portion of its output being exported to other countries. The Indian government has implemented various policies and programs to support and promote the textile industry, including the Scheme for Integrated Textile Parks and the Technology Upgradation Fund Scheme.

The Indian textile industry is also known for its handloom and handicraft textiles, which are produced in various regions across the country and are in high demand by buyers from around the world. These textiles are known for their unique designs and intricate patterns, and are considered to be an important aspect of India's cultural heritage.

The Indian textile industry also plays a vital role in the country's contemporary art scene, as textile is a medium that can be used to communicate cultural, political, and social messages. The use of textiles as an art medium highlights the rich cultural and traditional heritage of India and also helps to preserve traditional textile practices and techniques.

Overall, the Indian textile industry continues to be of ongoing significance for the Indian economy, culture and art scene. The traditional techniques and designs are being passed down through generations and are being incorporated into the contemporary art pieces and fashion, giving them a unique aesthetic. The industry continues to play a vital role in preserving the cultural heritage of India and promoting it globally.

Other Books Of The Author

1. The Moments When I Met God
2. Kashiyile Theertha Pathangal
3. GURU GYAN VANI
4. Abhiprerak Gita
5. ASSI SE JAIN GHAT TAK
6. Hopelessness of Arjuna
7. The Soul and It's True Nature
8. Sense of Action (Karma)
9. Action through Wisdom
10. Action through Wisdom
11. THEORY AND PRACTICAL OF EVERY ACTION
12. LOGICAL UNDERSTANDING OF THE SUPREME
13. THE IMPERISHABLE SUPREME
14. Yatra Nishadraj se Hanuman Ghat Tak
15. Yatra Karnatak Ghat se Raja Ghat Tak
16. Yatra Pandey Ghat se Prayagraj Ghat Tak
17. Yatra Ranjendra Prasad Ghat se Dattatreya Ghat Tak
18. YaatraSindhiya Ghat se Gwaliar Ghat Tak
19. Yatra Mangala Gauri Ghat se Hanuman Gadhi Ghat Tak
20. Yatra Gaay Ghat Se Nishad Ghat Tak
21. MAA GANGA, GHATEN EVM UTSAV
22. Ganga Arti Dev Deepavali evam Any Utsav
23. Potentials of Digitalized India
24. VEDIC CONSCIOUSNESS
25. A Brief Introduction to Vedic Science
26. Kashi ke Barah Jyotirling
27. IMPACT OF MOTIVATION
28. Let's have a Milky Way Journey
29. Color Therapy in a Nutshell

59. The Holistic Cow: A Look at the Physical, Spiritual, and Cultural Importance of Cows in India
60. Arts of Healing
61. Exploring the Divine
62. Understanding Five Elements
63. The Etymology of Ram
64. Symbols of India
65. Voice of Change (About Speeches of Great Men)
66. She Speaks (About Speeches of Great Women)
67. Patriotism on Celluloid – Brief About Patriotic Films
68. The Music of Motivation: A Brief Guide to Inspirational Film Songs
69. Unlocking the Secrets of the Dashopanishads
70. A Cultural Mosaic
71. Ancient Traditions, Modern Minds
72. Ecos of Ancient Wisdom
73. Beneath the Surface
74. From Temples to Ashrams
75. Sages of the Subcontinent
76. The Art of Healling (Ayurveda, Yoga & Naturopathy)
77. Indian Kitchen
78. The Festivals of India
79. The Indian Epics Retold
80. The Power of Mantras
81. The Indian River Ganges
82. The Indian Architecture
83. Rites of Passage
84. The Indian Silk Road
85. The Indian Literature
86. The Indian Villages
87. The Indian Folks & Crafts
88. The Way of Buddha
89. The Ramayan of Tulsidas

CONTACT

DR. JAGADEESH PILLAI

PhD in Vedic Science

Four Times Guinness World Record Holder

Winner of Mahatma Gandhi Vishwa Shanti Puraskar and
Global Peace Ambassador

Gemology, Astro & Vastu Consultant - Spiritual Counselor

Consultant for designing World Record Ideas

Efficient Tarot Card Reader

9839093003

myrichindia@gmail.com

drjagadeeshpillai@facebook

drjagadeeshpillai@instagram

jagadeeshpillai@youtube

www. JAGADEESHPILLAI.com

౸

|| LOKAHA SAMASTHAHA SUKHINO BHAVANTU ||

• 79 •